A special thanks to our featured Tiny Thinkers:
Edmond Palla
David Persing
James Palla
Maya Sanderson
Angelina Ferrucci

Carl Went to the Library
A Tiny Thinkers Book

Written by: M.J. Mouton
Illustrated by: Jezreel S. Cuevas
Edited by: David Smalley

©2018 Published by
Secular Media Group, LLC

Production Manager: David Smalley
Art Consultant: Deanie Mouton
Book Design: Courtney Benecke

Printed in China

US Library of Congress
ISBN: 9780998314792

Hi, I'm Hitch!

I've spent time with some amazing
Tiny Thinkers! Join me as we learn about
people and the science they discovered.
And see if you can spot me along the way,
as I tell you the story of Carl's real-life
adventure that changed the world!

CARL
WENT TO THE LIBRARY

Written by M.J. Mouton   Illustrated by Jezreel S. Cuevas

Foreword by   Michael Shermer

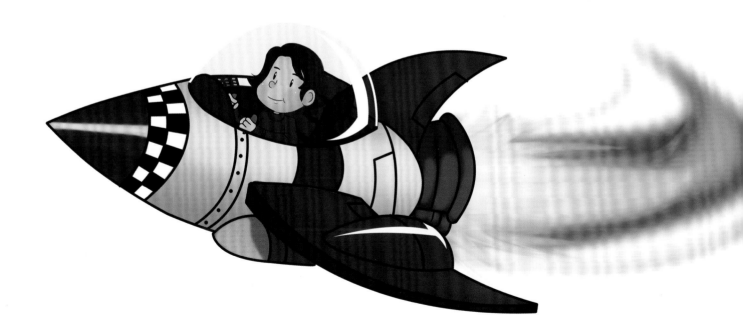

A Foreword by Michael Shermer

Hi, I'm Michael, the founder of Skeptic magazine, and Junior Skeptic magazine for kids.

Carl gave me the inspiration to make magazines devoted to scientific truths about reality. One of those inspiring stories was the first one I ever heard about Carl.

When I was in college, thinking about what I wanted to do with my life, that story inspired me to question and challenge beliefs and assumptions. It was about when Carl was a kid like you, and went to the library to ask for a book about the stars. The librarian first returned with a book about Hollywood celebrities—not the type of "stars" young Carl wanted to learn about!

Even at such a young age, little Carl had the courage and temerity to tell that librarian that he was interested in a different type of star, the type that lasts billions of years and burns brightly in the night sky, not the type that appears in movies and on TV.

That story is inspirational to me because most of what adults assume about children is wrong, and now that I'm an adult, I know that we need to look at the world through the curious eyes of a child and see the wonder and beauty and magnificence of nature as she really is, and not as we would like her to be.

Although Carl was famous because he was on TV—he became a "star" in the celebrity sense—that's not what was important to him. What mattered to Carl—and what made him burn brightly in the minds of so many of us young aspiring scientists and skeptics—was his love for the truth about reality.

Carl wanted to know what the universe is really like, and he wanted for kids like you to know, too!

—Michael Shermer, Publisher, *Skeptic Magazine*, writer for *Scientific American*, scientist and skeptic

Where should a **5**-year-old go,
when searching for an answer
that no one seems to know?

Carl had a question.
A BIG, WONDERFUL, AMAZING question!

He knew of a place that he could go.
A place with answers to questions
that no one seemed to know.

"I'll go to the library tomorrow,"
thought Carl in his bed,
as the question cut cartwheels
inside of his head.

Carl took a streetcar to the library.
He pretended to fly;
"I'm an airplane pilot, climbing up to the sky!"

He imagined he was flying to some far off places.
He passed people on sidewalks
with small smiles on BIG faces.

He flew around a parked car.
In the red paint he saw his reflection.

He then passed by a dog walking in his direction.

He did figure **8**'s around trees,
then he veered his plane sideways.
He watched out for cars in alleys and driveways.

He landed his plane at the library door,
as if he had flown to that same spot
many times before.

Carl walked in and said to the librarian,
"How do you do?" "I am fine, Carl," she said.
"What can I do for you?"

"I am looking for a book about stars,"
was Carl's polite request. "All the stars on TV?
I know the book that's the best!"

Blast off into
reading

"Not stars on TV, I need the twinkling lights
that cover the skies on the clearest of nights.
If you have such a book, it will surely help."

She returned in a flash with the right book.
Carl's eyes lit up, as he took a quick look.
A child's book about stars was exactly what he needed.
Carl found a small chair and he started to read it.

"What is a star?" Stars are made of gas.
They are BIG and bright. They are
blue, green, red, and seem to twinkle at night.

SUN

EARTH

VENUS

MERCURY

MARS

NEPTUNE   ERIS

JUPITER

URANUS

PLUTO

SATURN

CERES   MAKEMAKE

Carl had seen plenty of stars,
so those were things that he knew.
Then he found the answer to his question,
and more started to brew.

"The Sun is a REALLY close star. WOW!"
Carl's mind started to race.
"Every star in the sky is a sun for some place."

"Is the Sun really that BIG?" He thought as he read.
"OH MY!" The universe grew inside of Carl's
5-year-old head.

If every star is a sun,
then stars are REALLY FAR away.
Space became magnificent for
the first time that day.

The answer to his question reached out and grabbed his BIG imagination. "It never let go," would be Carl's explanation.

It was a fantastic wonder that revealed itself with one question, as Carl thought about space in the children's book section.

His imagination took over and Carl could not stop it.

The imaginary plane he flew to the library turned into a rocket!

He thought about traveling in the rocket to visit strange places, and maybe meet aliens on planets with HUGE smiles on small faces. He could see himself flying to Mars with its red reflection, as he passed by a comet flying in his direction.

He could do figure **8**'s around Earth
and Venus, or Jupiter and Saturn.

Or fly around Pluto, with one change of his rocket's pattern.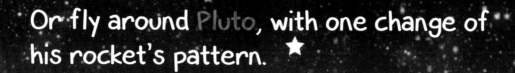

He could go so far into space that the Sun
would not seem so hot.
This BIG Earth that he lived on
would look like a dot.

Carl realized he lived in a very
BIG universe.
He had more questions to ask, so he
could learn how it worked.

With stars that could be counted in
BILLIONS upon BILLIONS,
His one little question could spark
MILLIONS upon MILLIONS.

When Carl had answers to many
of those questions,
he shared with everyone he met,
this amazing possession.

"Imagination can carry us to worlds that never were, but without imagination we go nowhere," is what Carl had learned.

Kids with BIG imaginations will dream of visiting far off places.
Maybe, they too, would think of aliens with smiles on their faces.

Maybe, you too, will be enlightened with a new cosmic obsession, that was inspired by the honest answer to a **5**-year-old's question.

Carl inspired us to see what the universe holds. All the things made from stars when those suns explode. Carl used that knowledge to inspire boys and girls. He taught people to love space and things out of this world.

THE END

Carl grew up to
be known as...

CARL SAGAN

1934–1996